Elephants
Living in Sanctuary

Photographs by Sangduen 'Lek' Chailert
Words by Scott McGregor

Acknowledgements

I would like to express my thanks to Kristin Foxlee for her work in putting this book together over the past couple of years. I would also like to thank Scott McGregor for writing the text. I am very grateful to all of my staff for their dedication to looking after the elephants and keeping the park running. I would like to thank all of the volunteers whose time, support and work on various projects over the years has made such a difference to the park and the lives of the elephants. A special thanks to Bert Von Roomer for being a light in the dark, and providing the funds to purchase the land on which Elephant Nature Park exists. Finally, I would like to express my deep gratitude to every person who has visited the park and all of the people and organisations that have made donations over the years. Without the support of so many people who have shown that they care about elephants, Elephant Nature Park would not be possible. So from me, and on behalf of the elephants, thank you!

Elephants - Living in Sanctuary
First edition published in January 2008
Second edition published in March 2009

Photographs by Sangduen Chailert
Words by Scott McGregor
Design by Kristin Foxlee

For more information contact Elephant Nature Park at
1 Ratmakka Road, T. Phrasingh, A. Muang
Chiang Mai 50200 Thailand
Tel: +66 (0) 53 272 855   Fax: +66 (0) 53 270 884
Website: www.saveelephant.org
Email: info@saveelephant.org

ISBN: 978-974-04-1799-6
Printed in Thailand by Amarin Printing & Publishing

www. saveelephant.org

Background

For centuries people have been attracted to the elephant. Fascinated by its size, strength, intelligence and sheer majesty, the elephant holds a special place in our imaginations. Elephants have always played an honoured role in Asian society as symbols of national pride, religious reverence and tradition, as well as serving as beasts of burden with seemingly endless reserves of strength.

The reality is that humans have destroyed most of this beloved animal's habitat, killed them for their tusks, worked them literally to death and forced them to perform for our entertainment. It is estimated that today there are probably fewer than 30,000 elephants remaining in Asia - one tenth the number living in Africa. Approximately half of these elephants are living in captivity. Our determination to domesticate one of the world's largest and most intelligent animals has resulted in a centuries old tradition known as *phajaan*. During this ritual, young elephants are dragged from their mother's side, placed in a cage and brutalised until their will and spirit are broken, accepting man as their master and a life based on fear.

Elephants working in logging are often underfed, overworked and have been known to be given amphetamines to push them beyond normal levels of endurance, sometimes resulting in horrific accidents. Many elephants are forced to walk crowded city streets to earn their keep by begging for overpriced bananas paid for by onlookers. This is a risky occupation where elephants are sometimes hit by cars, become sick from drinking polluted water and inhaling exhaust fumes, as well as suffer damage to their ears, eyes and feet. In seemingly innocuous elephant camps set up for the enjoyment of tourists, there is often considerable suffering behind the scenes. Elephants are frequently beaten with an *ankush* (a curved, metal hook used to train and discipline elephants), forced to carry tourists while heavily pregnant, and trained to perform demeaning tricks.

The 200 or so photographs appearing in this book were taken by Sangduen 'Lek' Chailert, founder of Elephant Nature Park and show a happier side of life for a group of lucky elephants rescued over the past 16 years. Elephant Nature Park has also given temporary shelter, medical treatment and love to countless more elephants throughout Thailand. Many of the elephants arrive at the park with painful memories fresh in their minds but soon discover that their fortunes have taken a turn for the better. Often for the first time in their lives these elephants are free to choose their own herd and roam the expanse of the park, unchained. In this sanctuary they experience a kinder world, where they are loved and honoured as the amazing beings they are. Here, their fears start to dissolve and their wounds, both physical and mental, begin to heal.

The images presented in this book are of elephants that have been given the opportunity to reawaken their spirit and simply, to enjoy life. They show the playful nature of elephants emerging in the safe environment of the park, where their individual personalities and quirks find expression. Many of the photographs are of young elephants that have never known the brutality of *phajaan and* are being taught with love and food rewards instead of pain. This pioneering work being carried out by Lek and her mahouts (elephant handlers) is revealing that *phajaan* is an unnecessary evil and that a more enlightened approach to training elephants is possible. Elephant Nature Park is a true success story. More and more people are choosing to observe elephants interacting in a relatively natural environment, rather than riding them or watching them perform circus tricks.

If attitudes change, then there may be hope for the future of the Asian elephant, otherwise it seems likely that their natural habitat will continue to disappear in man's destructive wake and those in captivity will remain sacred but exploited. It is hoped that this book will help to bring greater awareness to the perilous situation of the Asian elephant and provide insight into the nature of this extraordinary, yet endangered species. Just like us, elephants deserve the right to freedom and happiness.

A Note from Lek

When I first met many of the elephants seen in the photographs of this book I could hardly believe the state they were in. They had such vacant eyes, barely registering my presence, and would even refuse food. The unnatural conditions that they were living in had pushed them to the edge of desperation and their level of suffering was too much to bear. Many were withdrawn and had all but given up on life. They were like the living dead.

We rescued these elephants and brought them to the park to start a new life. We wanted to give them the chance to live freely in an environment close to their natural habitat, without having to work, and amongst people who love and respect them. At the park the elephants are free to choose a family, form small herds and for the first time feel they have a real home. These amazing creatures need a place to heal. I believe that love can heal anything. We give them the opportunity to be elephants again, which means to live with love, to play, to have fun and be happy.

Over the years I have observed that elephants are quite refined in the way they relate to each other and structure their society. Elephants have a strong sense of duty within the herd, especially when it comes to protecting and caring for their young. They are mostly peace loving animals and bonds between elephants often last a lifetime.

In many ways, elephants are not that much different from humans. They are naturally very expressive animals and are highly emotional, social and intelligent. Communication between elephants is very sophisticated and operates on levels that we only partially understand. They love to have fun and even have a sense of humour, play jokes on each other and can be seen smiling and giggling. This behaviour only surfaces when elephants are given the freedom to live without fear. I hope that the photographs in this book reveal what beautiful, complex and often joyful beings elephants are when they are allowed to be.

Left: Pupia tries to push Dok Mai into the river while his mother, Mae Toh Koh sips the cool water. Mae Toh Koh's name means Long Legs. Her baby, Pupia, was born undersized and weak because she was working as a trekking elephant during her pregnancy and did not get enough rest or food. They arrived at the park in January, 2006. Both were in poor condition, but with the help of park staff and volunteers, soon recovered their health.

Right: Mae Yui, Pupia, Dok Mai and Dok Ngern look wonderful in profile during a late afternoon bath in the river.

Left: Pu Pah (whose name means Golden Rock), attracts the attention of his two young friends, Hope and Jungle Boy, who seem intent on keeping him in the mud.

Right: Hope, also known as Yod Doi (meaning Mountain Top) and Jungle Boy, also known as Tong Suk (meaning Golden Happiness) have a wild time in the mud together. Hope came to the park in 2002 as an 18 month old male after his mother died. Jungle Boy, who is a year younger, arrived in 2003. In these photos they are four and five years old. A bond formed between these two elephants on their very first meeting and their antics are a daily event at the park.

Left: Tong Jan, Aura, Kanoon and Jo Baan scramble for sticks of sugarcane, a popular treat amongst the elephants.

Right: Pretty, one year old Tong Jan stands between logs washed up on the river bank, her face painted with mud. Tong Jan, whose name means Golden Moon, was born on Valentine's Day, 2005. Tong Jan narrowly escaped being sold to a circus in Pattaya, and instead was rescued and brought to the park along with her mother, Mae Bua Tong, when she was just a few months old.

Tong Jan, Aura and Pupias' lives revolve around playing, eating and sleeping. Their unrestrained exuberance is a reflection of how safe they feel in their environment. On the left Dok Mai joins her friends.

Hope and Pu Pah frolic in the river. Hope has no fear of Pu Pah, who is 15 years his senior and they love to test their strength against each other. They are often the last two elephants out of the river, relishing every moment.

Above: Little Aura pins down her buddy, Tong Jan, in the hot sand.

Right: Tong Jan wrestles Aura to the ground and Kanoon adds his weight to the stack. Their mums stay close by to make sure the fun does not end in tears.

Left: Towering above, Pu Pah gently hooks his powerful trunk under Hope's chin. Jungle Boy daydreams in the soft mud. Despite already going through his first musth (a state of increased sexual activity accompanied by aggression in male elephants), Pu Pah seems intent on protracting his childhood.

Above: Pu Pah slides into the mud pit, pushing aside Jungle Boy.

Right: Pu Pah plasters himself in the slippery mud, while Hope nudges him from behind.

Left & Above: Pupia clambers onto Aura's back and holds on with his trunk. Aura does her best to maintain her balance on the uneven surface of the ditch, but with Tong Jan weighing in from behind, her position looks precarious.

Right: Aura defiantly blocks Pupia, allowing Tong Jan to continue her blinding run towards the goal, or so it seems. These three young elephants never tire of each other's company.

Left: Kanoon salutes the sun, casting sand over his back after bathing in the river. This is a favourite elephant ritual.

Top: Tong Jan smiles playfully while entertaining herself in the sand.

Above: Aura takes possession of an old piece of bamboo washed up on the river bank.

Left: Tong Jan and Kanoon probe each other familiarly with their trunks.

Right: Hope, Jungle Boy, No Na Mi and Mae Boon Na indulge in a mud bath together. The mud nourishes their skin and protects it from the sun.

Far Left: Tong Jan, wild eyed with excitement, drinks from the river.

Left: Jungle Boy rests his trunk affectionately on Tong Jan's head.

Above: Mae Bua Tong, which means Golden Lotus, and Tong Jan immerse themselves in the cool water. They are framed by Thai who stands in the foreground. At the tender age of three, Thai was taken from her mother and sold into tourism where she was made to perform in shows with a travelling circus. At 12, she was walking the busy streets of Bangkok as a begging elephant. She was rescued and brought to the park in her middle age, where she quickly made friends and restored her health. She now enjoys playing 'aunty' to baby Tong Jan. The term aunty is used to describe the maternal role that some female elephants undertake, if accepted by a mother and calf.

Left: Somboon, Pupia, Dok Mai, Mae Yui and Mae Toh Koh look very much the happy family as they graze in the late afternoon.

Right & Above: Mae Toh Koh and Malai Tong entwine their trunks during an intimate moment. Malai Tong's back left foot was badly injured by a land mine in 2003, while working in illegal logging. After eight months in recovery she was put to work as a street begging elephant in Bangkok and later Isaan. In 2005 she was rescued and brought to the park where she formed a strong friendship with Mae Toh Koh, who welcomed her help in looking after her baby, Pupia.

Left: Kanoon faces the camera straight legged and a little menacingly. Behind, Tong Jan flings sand, accompanied by Jo Baan.

Right: Aura, Tong Jan and Kanoon party on the beach, chaperoned by Mae Boon.

Below: Aura lies in the sand, trunk raised, amidst the dust. Her mother, Mae Boon flaps her ears and scuffs the ground.

Above: Tong Jan gives Aura an oral examination with her trunk while she enjoys a luxurious mud bath.

Right: Tong Jan happily wallows in the mud, providing entertainment for Mae Elu, Aura and Mae Boon.

Mae Boon gave birth to Aura in 2005. Both mother and baby were weak and malnourished at the time and were brought to the park at their owner's request to give them a chance to recover their health. Mae Elu is about 55 years old and has strong maternal instincts, acting as freelance aunty to all of the baby elephants at the park. While working in the logging trade, Mae Elu gave birth to three babies, but only one is still alive today, and she is currently employed in a trekking camp.

Left: Mae Elu, Aura and Mae Boon hang out together by the logs on the beach.

Above: Pupia and Aura look very cute in profile, with their spiky, juvenile hair clearly visible.

Right: Pupia and Tong Jan mess around in the sand. Somboon and Thai stand behind.

Left: Elephant ecstasy: Pupia, Tong Jan, Aura and Malai Tong slosh around in the mud pit, coating themselves in the chocolate brown slush.

Above: Pupia, Tong Jan and Malai Tong continue to muck around in the mud, heads down.

Above: Kanoon innocently tries to mount Tong Jan, with Aura providing an inconvenient obstacle below.

Left: Tong Jan delivers a playful kick to Kanoon while lying on her side in the sand.

Left: Tong Jan does her impression of a whale spraying water from its blow hole.

Below: Tong Jan appears to be smiling as she and Aura dust themselves with sand, fresh from their bath. Mae Boon looks on with motherly affection.

Left: Pu Pah affectionately drapes his long trunk over Hope's head. His affections are not limited to his male buddies. In fact, Pu Pah is the resident Casanova of the park and is known for his amorous adventures with the ladies.

Above & Right: Three month old Pupia embraces his mother, Mae Toh Koh, in the river.

Left: Mae Perm and Jokia cross their trunks while foraging for food in the jungle. Mae Perm, whose name means Most Lucky, was the first elephant rescued by Lek in 1992 and asserts her authority by chasing new females around the park, much to their bewilderment. Jokia was rescued in 1998, having spent years working in an illegal logging camp. She lost her baby while working under dangerous conditions and fell into a deep depression, refusing to work. This provoked the wrath of her desperate mahout who hit her in the eye with a rock using a sling shot. Jokia naturally became more resentful and was sold, only to be shot in her remaining good eye with an arrow, leaving her in a world of darkness. One day Lek heard Jokia trumpeting angrily in the jungle where she was being forced to work, and so began the negotiation for her release. Jokia and Mae Perm are now inseparable best friends. Mae Perm sees for Jokia and is on the constant look out for her, communicating her position with low, reassuring rumbles and warning her of approaching strangers.

Above: Jokia opens her mouth wide and reaches for fresh foliage with her long muscular trunk.

Top Right: Jokia improvises a sun hat from a large banana leaf.

Right: Mae Perm extends her trunk to grab some more bamboo leaves, a favourite delicacy of elephants.

Above & Right: Pupia
practices elephant yoga
on the edge of the mud pit.
Dok Ngern swings her tail
and watches from behind.

Above: Dok Ngern gives in to gravity and rests her legs.

Left: Jungle Boy shows off his rolls of baby fat while on his knees, leaning nose first into the mud pit.

Left: A magnificent sight: covered in red earth and foliage, Mae Elu, Mae Toh Koh, Pupia, Dok Mai, Mae Yui and Dok Ngern gather on the beach before descending into the river.

Above: Hope and Malai Tong tenderly press their heads together.

Above: Pupia wears an undeniable smile as he clings to Aura, who is busy nuzzling Tong Jan. Sri Nuan stands behind.

Top Right: Pupia shows off for the camera, raising himself on the back of Tong Jan in the river.

Bottom Right: More antics in the river from the dynamic trio: Pupia on Aura, Aura on Tong Jan, Tong Jan on the riverbed.

Left: Phu Pa gets sandwiched between Hope and Jungle Boy. Mae Perm and Jokia pass on by.

Above: Hope, looking incredibly plump, playfully climbs onto Phu Pa's back.

Right: Phu Pa straightens his front legs, preparing to lift his considerable frame from the mud, with Hope leaning on him behind.

Above: Hope and Jungle Boy fool around in the mud pit. Somboon lets the mud bake on her back under the fierce heat of the sun. Somboon, who is in her late 40's, spent much of her life begging on the streets. Her eyesight and hearing are both damaged from the exposure to the bright lights, pollution and city noise. She came to the park in August, 2003. Somboon used to hang out with Hope a lot until the arrival of Tong Jan, with whom she quickly became enamoured. Now she divides her time between them but still takes time out to be alone.

Above: Hope and Jungle Boy engage in a friendly spar. Their play fights sometimes get quite rough causing minor injuries to each other. Jungle Boy is a bold and mischievous young elephant. He is cared for by his diligent and loving aunty, Mae Keow, who sometimes sends Hope on his way when he gets too boisterous.

When Hope was first rescued as an orphaned elephant, he was angry, unpredictable and frightened. Lek patiently gained his trust by sneaking into his pen in the dark to hug and caress him while he slept. She knew she had won Hope's trust when he came to her one night and allowed her to stroke and comfort him until he fell asleep.

Left & Above: Tong Jan lies in the hot sand with Aura's foot placed lightly on her belly. Mae Toh Koh and Mae Bua Tong stand over them,. their trunks curled contemplatively. Somboon reaches out with her long, speckled trunk.

Mae Bua Tong, who used to work in trekking, and her baby, Tong Jan, came to the park in 2005. She made friends easily and a new social group made up of Somboon, Thai and Mae Elu quickly formed, all vying for the job of aunty to Tong Jan. Mae Bua Tong is a great mother with a big heart, and happily welcomes other elephants into her herd.

Kanoon and Tong Jan play piggyback on the beach. As Tong Jan's aunty, Somboon maintains a watchful eye.

Left: Jungle Boy emerges from the undergrowth, trunk to the forest floor, sniffing out favoured plants.

Below: Hope is in his element, foraging in the lush jungle. Somewhat the 'Park Inspector', Hope always makes it his business to investigate new arrivals, whether they be elephants, buffalo, people or machinery.

Above & Right: Jungle Boy amuses himself with an old car tyre, effortlessly knocking it around with his trunk and feet.

Left: Pupia appears to be in danger of sinking into the mud with Tong Jan and Dok Ngern coming to his rescue. In truth the slosh is only a couple of feet deep.

Above: Pupia climbs aboard Dok Ngern, while she awkwardly attempts to raise herself.

Right: Pupia face-plants the soft earth, his wet, chubby backside glistening in the sun. Tong Jan and Aura gather nearby.

Left: Pupia's hairy head pops up in the river next to Sri Nuan and eight year old Dok Ngern. Dok Ngern and Sri Nuan arrived at the park together in January, 2006, saved from a life of begging on the streets. They quickly made friends and became part of the family group that includes Malai Tong, Mae Toh Koh and Pupia. Dok Ngern is fiercely protective of her little adopted brother. Sri Nuan, who is easily identified by her large head and broad shoulders, has become a loving aunty to baby Pupia.

Right: Sri Nuan scratches her foot on a log, showing off her impressive nails. Pupia uses the same log to scratch his belly. Behind, Dok Ngern swings her trunk.

Left: Under the forest canopy, Mae Keow, Jungle Boy and Lilly forage for food, wearing a camouflage of earth and vines. Lilly is known for her gentle nature, which is remarkable given the exploitation to which she has been subjected. She was fed amphetamines to keep her working day and night until her inevitable collapse. In late 1995, Lilly was rescued and began her long road to recovery. Today she is a kindly, unhurried elephant and much loved by all at the park. Mae Keow, who was a logging elephant, had been chained virtually all of her adult life. When she came to the park in 1998, she celebrated her first taste of freedom by hiding out in the jungle for three days. Mae Keow is a small elephant with a big personality.

Above: Jokia enjoys snacking on juicy banana stalks in the jungle.

Left: Aura runs through the mud pit, ears flapping, in a mock charge. Aura is a clever, strong-willed young elephant who is not afraid to express her feelings.

Right: Tong Jan slips and slides in the mud while Aura leans on her with her trunk. Mae Elu observes their antics.

Above: Pupia makes a grab for Aura's kinked tail as he slides down the side of the ditch under the weight of Tong Jan.

Right: The three musketeers: Tong Jan, Aura and Pupia are in a huddle. Once this trio begin to play, virtually nothing can distract them from their fun.

Left & Above: Kanoon, accompanied by his friend, Tong Jan, rolls around in the grass and unsteadily gets to his feet. Mae Bua Tong stands behind.

Right: Tong Jan affectionately leans into Kanoon, who reveals the pink tip of his trunk.

In these photos Tong Jan, Aura, Mae Elu and Thai get down and dirty in the soft red earth, which powders much of their bodies.

Above & Left: Hope makes a fountain with his trunk. Pu Pah immerses himself in the cool water behind.

Right: Phu Pa and Hope, who are both passionate about aquatic sports, constantly reinvent ways of having fun in the river.

Boon Rod, Hope and Jungle
Boy in full flight as they race
each other to the river.

Left: Pupia scrambles up his mother's leg, made slippery in the river. Mae Toh Koh leans back on Sri Nuan for support.

Above: Tong Jan curls her trunk around Aura. Thai and Mae Boon form pillars left and right with Somboon and Mae Bua Tong in the shadows.

Top Left: Hope, with everlasting curiosity, burrows into a stack of debris washed up on the bank of the river.

Bottom Left: Jungle Boy presses his face into the soft mud, like a pig searching for truffles.

Right: Hope and Pu Pah seem to pose for the camera. Hope makes sure he's in the picture, leaning hard on Pu Pah.

Above: Medo curls her trunk and scratches her head ponderously while Mae Mai stands behind. Medo is the most obviously disabled elephant at the park, having sustained two terrible injuries. The first was to her left ankle, which was broken when a heavy log fell on her while working in the jungle on the Thai-Burmese border. Unable to use Medo for work, it was decided that she should breed, so her owner tried coupling her with a huge bull elephant. At the time, Medo was chained by all 4 legs and being in musth, the bull acted aggressively and pinned her to the ground with his full weight, breaking her back. Medo fought for her life and despite her severe deformity now lives a satisfying existence at the park.

Right: Mae Bua Tong reveals the amazing dexterity of her trunk.

Tong Jan, Aura and Pupia amuse themselves easily, messing around in the ditch on a sunny afternoon. Twenty-one year old Malai Tong supervises the fun in her capacity as aunty. Jungle Boy stands in the distance, a glint of mischief in his eye. Above, Dok Ngern watches from the right while Mae Elu appears on the left.

Aura tries to pin down Tong Jan while she squirms and twists in the soft mud.

Left: Mae Kham Sai and Hope entwine trunks in an affectionate embrace. When Mae Kham Sai arrived at the park in 2004, she was so covered in the purple antiseptic used to treat her wounds that she became known as 'The Purple Elephant'. Eventually her position at the park was secured. Her health has much recovered since her arrival, though she remains blind in one eye following a crop raiding incident earlier in her life. Mae Kham Sai is one of the few female elephants who chooses to be alone rather than belonging to a social group, though occasionally she accepts an offering of friendship from Hope and Mae Elu.

Below: Hope's trunk stretches up finding Mae Kham Sai's mouth while she takes in the scent on the breeze.

Top Left: Khum Min arrived at the park in August, 2003, having worked in logging for decades and then trekking. Abscesses formed on his back as a result of carrying a seat for tourists for several hours a day. His condition became so chronic that his owner decided to sell him. Since coming to the park he is much healthier and regularly goes into musth.

Bottom Left: Mae Lanna and Dok Ngern lock trunks in the river. Mae Lanna arrived at the park in February, 2007, with a long work history that included giving rides to tourists on Koh Phi Phi, rubber tree logging in Phang Nga province and street begging in Surin. She was very reserved when she first arrived at the park but has recently become more sociable.

Right: Max, thought to be one of the tallest elephants in Thailand, is seen here in his characteristic pose, leaning back, taking the weight off his front legs. In 1999 Max was hit by an 18 wheel logging truck on his way home from street begging one night. He was pushed along the ground for several feet, leaving him with terrible injuries, including a broken front right leg. When he was rescued and brought to the park in 2002, Max was in a weak state but soon began a slow recovery. He does not belong to any family group, which is quite typical of males. A gentle giant, Max ambles around the park, mostly keeping a low profile, though he does attract the attention of many female admirers.

Above: Pupia tentatively practices his mounting technique with Aura on a hot, dusty afternoon.

Left: Pupia demands attention from Aura, who responds by pulling a bizarre face.

Right: Aura shakes her head from side to side while Pupia wheels around behind her, planning a surprise attack. Pupia still has the innocence of youth and is rather clumsy at times. Aura beams with confidence and is a bit of a trickster.

Above: Hope elegantly steps out of the mud pit.

Left: Faa Sai, Pupia and Tong Jan stand together conspiratorially while Aura breaks away from the group.

Right: Pupia and Hope get up close and personal.

Above: Hope emerges from a thick grove of bamboo and continues to forage in the jungle.

Above Left: Mae Boon keeps feeding during the climb up the mountain. Aura and Somboon follow in her footsteps.

Left: Mae Elu looks magnificent in the shadows of the forest canopy, her mouth stuffed with bamboo leaves.

Right: Mae Perm and Jokia enjoy a feast of banana stalks in the cool, lush jungle.

Left: Boon Rod, in a euphoric
moment, raises her trunk and
opens her mouth in a wide smile
while bathing in the river.

Above: Tong Jan happily covers
her head with sand and pebbles.
Tong Jan is somewhat of a deva
and can be rather selective when
it comes to food and friends.

Tong Jan and Aura are completely at home in the water and love to dunk each other, forcing the use of their trunks as snorkels.

Above: Pupia rolls around in the mud at Aura's feet while Tong Jan enters from the right. In the height of the dry season the elephants love to hang by the mud pool.

Right: Tong Jan, Pupia, Sri Nuan, Aura and Dok Ngern are head to head in the mud pit. Pupia looks particularly pleased with himself.

Left: Boon Rod sits dog-like and stretches her trunk while Tong Jan attempts to squeeze her way under Thai's belly. Behind, Jungle Boy elegantly raises one leg, his trunk dangling on a log.

Above: Aura looks very much the baby, playing in the sand. Her mother, Mae Boon, stands protectively behind.

Left: Pupia and Aura look disconcerted by Tong Jan's exuberant pose. Jungle Boy's small tusk breaks the surface of the water close by. Dok Ngern makes her way upstream.

Right: For Dok Ngern, Pupia, Aura, Jungle Boy and Tong Jan, bath time is always an occasion for some lighthearted fun.

Left: Pupia plays dead, but Aura is unconvinced. Mae Bua Tong stands over them while Thai walks on by.

Above: Assembled here in various poses are Dok Ngern, Mae Toh Koh, Tong Jan, Pupia and Sri Nuan.

Hope and Malai Tong enjoy a friendly spar. Not always an expression of aggression, this activity can help to reinforce bonds between elephants.

Hope and Malai Tong continue to spar in the grassy field. Malai Tong is 14 years Hope's senior and over the past couple of years they have formed a close bond.

Top Left: Tong Jan, Pupia and Aura get down and dirty in the squidgy mud.

Bottom Left: Pupia attempts to leap out of the mud pit. Aura, Tong Jan and Mae Elu hang around for a little more fun. Jungle Boy and Hope spar in the background.

Above & Right: Malai Tong delivers a friendly kick to Pupia while exiting the mud pit. Aura and Tong Jan teeter on the edge.

Boon Khum enjoys a workout, kicking the old tyre around. Above, he is joined by Mae Boon, who is fond of his company. BK, as he is affectionately known, is the dominant bull elephant at the park and is easily identified by his powerful physique and one remaining tusk. While on a break from logging in the jungle, a poacher drugged BK and removed one of his tusks with a chainsaw. The cut was made so high in the greed for ivory that a terrible infection developed. Fearing the poacher's return, his owner cut off most of his other tusk. Many years later the infection has not completely healed, though BK enjoys much improved health.

Above & Right: Pupia and Tong Jan trumpet and hurl sand from the beach, most of it landing on Aura, who stands behind.

Left: Tong Jan, Pupia and Dok Ngern make white water as they race through the shallows. Somboon and Hope follow at a more leisurely pace.

Right: Pupia is caught in a moment of pure excitement as he climbs onto Tong Jan. Behind, Jungle Boy rolls back into the water.

Top Left: Pupia and Tong Jan continue their games in the river. Dok Ngern's head pops up behind.

Bottom Left: Dok Ngern, Aura, Tong Jan and Pupia are shoulder to shoulder, looking a little hippo-like. Somboon, a buxom beauty in her 40's, forms the backdrop. She has little ears and chubby cheeks, which give her an endearing, permanent smile.

Above: Aura and Tong Jan are kissed by the early morning sun as they feed on the lush grass together.

Above: New arrival, Tong Daeng, is warmly greeted by Dok Ngern, who gently drapes her trunk over his head, while keeping a respectful distance.

Hope and Jungle Boy are the dynamic duo of the park and spend much of their day sparring, playing in the river or in the mud pit. Neither of them have had to endure the *phajaan* ritual or life as a working elephant and it shows in their unfettered playfulness. Hope is a likeable elephant with a huge personality and will surely have many female admirers as he matures. He is friendly with people and enjoys showing off when the mood takes him. Jungle Boy is a daring elephant, who is shaping up to be a bit of a stud. He proudly displays his juvenile tusks and can be seen sharpening them to fine points.

Left: Jungle Boy stands defiantly before Medo and Mae Lanna, who he loves to tease. Mae Lanna was very shy when she first came to the park but has recently befriended Medo, and these two elephants are now great companions.

Above: Jungle Boy and Mae Lanna hook trunks.

Right: Despite her disability, when Medo has had enough of Jungle Boy she lets him know with a few playful bites and shoves.

Hope and Pu Pah are caught here in some dramatic poses as they wrestle each other in a friendly contest of strength.

130

Left & Right: Mae Boon Ma enjoys kicking the old tyre around and then takes time out, sitting on a log by the river. She satisfies five of the seven criteria used to distinguish a white elephant from an ordinary elephant including having pink skin, white tail hair and white nails. Unbeknownst to Mae Boon Ma, white elephants are regarded as sacred and are highly revered in Thailand. Mae Boon Ma has recently become an aunty to baby Tong Tae, satisfying her strong maternal instincts.

Below: Sri Nuan, Mae Tong Dee and Mae Boon Ma display their curvaceous butts with little Tong Tae peering through the arch made by his elders.

Top Left: Aura, Tong Jan and Kanoon make an elephant train on the beach while Mae Boon catches a scent on the wind.

Far Left: Delicately balanced, Kanoon pauses, his path blocked by Tong Jan's head.

Bottom Left: Pupia scrambles over a log on the beach.

Above: Framed by a blue sky and undulating hills, Thai, Tong Jan, Pupia, Dok Mai and Somboon gather around the sun-bleached logs.

135

Above: Sri Nuan dribbles water from her trunk. Malai Tong and Aura relax in the water behind.

Top Right: Pupia, Dok Ngern, Sri Nuan, Mae Yui and Mae Toh Koh enjoy a communal bath.

Bottom Right: Pupia drinks from the river, imitating his mother, but struggling to reach his mouth with his small trunk.

Far Right: Mae Yui and Mae Toh Koh keep each other company in the river.

Left: Kanoon shares a joke with Tong Jan after covering themselves with sand.

Above: Kanoon amuses himself by rolling around in the sand.

Right: Tong Jan, Aura and Kanoon scatter sand to the wind.

Left: Tong Jan, Pupia, Aura and Dok Ngern line up on the edge of the mud pit like the front row of a rugby team. When Dok Ngern arrived at the park she was so full of fear that even the sight of a tree stump startled her, causing her to shriek. Hope and Jungle Boy were immediately interested in befriending her, being around the same age, but she was too intimidated by them. Instead, she formed close ties with Pupia, who was a fraction her size. She is a more relaxed elephant today however, and does not hesitate to join in unrestrained play with the other young elephants. There is little evidence of Dok Ngern's troubled past and she has become a fun loving elephant with a sweet nature.

Above: Dok Ngern buries her trunk in the mud. Pupia and Aura can't resist joining in.

Left: Jo Baan takes her two week old baby, Kanoon, for a stroll to the river.

Above: Tong Tae runs to keep up with mother, Mae Tong Dee, as she gathers grass in the pouring rain.

Right: Tong Tae looks enchanting with his perfectly formed ears, large innocent eyes and mud powdered trunk.

Left: Jungle Boy sends a tyre skyward with a flick of his trunk. Pu Pah watches in anticipation from behind.

Below: Pu Pah deftly balances the tyre on his trunk. Jungle Boy saunters over for a piece of the action.

Right: Pu Pah is caught here just before launching the tyre with a swing of his trunk. Pu Pah and Jungle Boy happily spend hours throwing the tyre around and have become quite expert at controlling it with their powerful trunks.

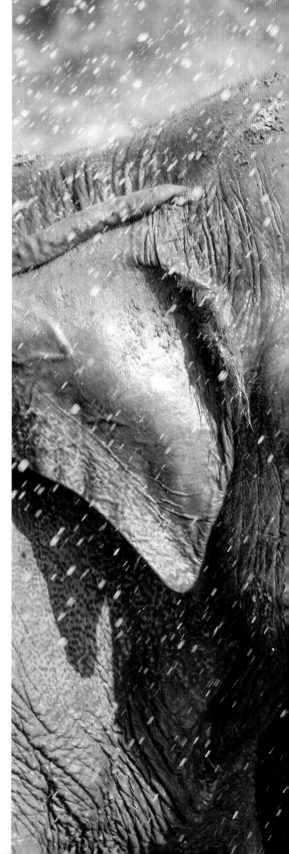

Above: Mae Boon, Aura, and Mae Boon Ma drink from the river, their muddied skin bronzed in the soft light of the late afternoon.

Right: Mae Toh Koh looks beautiful, eyes shut tight, as she showers herself with sparkling river water.

Above: Sri Nuan looks very impressive against the backdrop of a blue sky. Pupia stays close by his aunty's side as they walk through the field.

Right: Mae Bua Tong leads Tong Jan and Aura through the lush green grass towards the river. Mae Elu, Thai, and Somboon amble along behind.